Suzanne, with lots n love and
every blessing.

Elinor Kapp

Unlike the Swan

Elinor Kapp

OPENING CHAPTER
Creative Media

First Printing, 2023

ISBN: 1-904958-77-X
EAN: 9781904958772

published by:

Opening Chapter

openingchapter.com

My grateful thanks to Derec Jones and Rhian Jones, for their editorial and artistic expertise, without which this book could not have been created.

This book is dedicated to my wonderful family.

Rupert and Erika Rawnsley
And their sons Alex and Nate

and

Amanda and Jon Foster
And their sons Freddy and Frankie

Also, to the memory of my dear late husband,
Prof. Ken Rawnsley, 1926 – 1992

INTRODUCTION

I learned to read at an early age and it became my main activity and amusement as a child. I also wrote a lot of poems, which was encouraged in school, particularly at Walthamstow Hall where I had very good teachers. The poems in this book, however, are ones written much later in my adult life.

Some of the poems here were written in the desperate sorrow after the death of my little boy Andrew, in 1967 {as described in my Memoirs} However, others are written in the first person but relate to experiences I have not had myself. In these I have used my imagination to 'live in' to all sorts of people, and even inanimate objects. Far from being some sort of 'Cultural Appropriation', as seems to be a new and regrettably negative idea, these poems represent a vital part of my work, indeed of my whole life.

This is not new nor any sort of unusual attitude. We surely all know that no one can develop an empathic understanding of how other human beings feel and behave without an imaginative 'living into' their lives?

When I began to study medicine, particularly psychological conditions, I consciously used this imaginative ability to 'live into' the life of each human being who consulted me. That enabled me to feel some idea of what they felt and offer appropriate help. It was never taught at medical school, but I later found out that this was a recognised way in post-Freudian psychology, and known as 'phenomenology'.

So welcome to my world, in which one can become for a few moments another being and investigate the mixed and muddled emotions, particularly those surrounding Love, and sex.

The poems explain themselves, but in case the reader would also like to learn what I had found, or find the verses difficult, I have followed some of the poems with a 'NOTE'.

A recent journey by train carried me back through my past, when for the first time in many years I found myself approaching Croydon, the town in which I had grown up. I stared out at the suburban streets eagerly looking for the old water tower that marked the end of my road.

I remembered lying in bed as a small girl listening to the shriek of the steam trains suddenly dropping a tone as they passed, like greetings from iron dragons. From where did they come and to what strange places would they go? My bedroom window looked over the park and the railway to the town. In the distance I could see the town hall and blocks of flats. Further away on the skyline the strange, truncated, curved cones of Cooling Towers.

I had watched them all through my childhood, in all seasons, times and weathers. Sometimes they floated above dawn clouds, as transparent and ethereal as fairy towers. At other times they were as menacing as Gormanghast or Childe

Harold's dark tower.

I never told anyone of these things. I already knew that flats and cooling towers were not among the things admired or considered as Art. "Real Art" was oil painting, done almost always by men and appearing miraculously as finished pieces in galleries. "Almost Art" was watercolours and drawings that my mother and aunts did as a hobby. I tried these, and quickly gave up, discouraged by my inability to achieve realism, as so many children do.

I am not blaming the adults for this, nor the art teachers; these were the prevailing attitudes of the time. Far from suppressing my creativity my mother encouraged me, spending patient hours as I created a whole village out of matchboxes. When I was twelve years old she helped me design and embroider a tray cloth with Noah's Ark in the middle and pairs of animals round the edge, finishing little bits when I got bored and never expecting me to unpick minor mistakes.

The embroidered patterns she made on curtains and bed cover seams were more a relaxation than a creative activity. All these things seemed like a woman's secret activity, not important in the "real world", but inhabiting a special place between my mother and myself, a part of our relationship, cosy and warm, full of quiet pleasure, given and received.

When I was six, with chickenpox, I woke to find a knitted rabbit in a football jersey by my bed. When I was seven and had to have all my hair shaved off she knitted me two pixie hoods, in red and black, in a vain attempt to ward off teasing at school. She helped me make clay models for Grandpa and a patchwork cushion for Grandma, cherished by the recipients for many years.

I now recognize that special space, that area between my mother and myself. It is the "Sacred Space", spoken of as occasionally occurring between the voice of the singer and the ear of the hearer, between the artist and the viewer, the actor and the audience. It is sacred because it is set apart, because it requires relationship, because it cannot take place without attention from both sides and it is also there in all religions, between priests and congregation.

It occurred occasionally between my father and I when we talked of intellectual matters and when he encouraged me in my medical career, but it occurred between my mother and I when she encouraged my creativity, when I was ill and cared for by her, when we talked about women's secrets – menstruation, sex, dates, clothes, fantasy, and fairy tales.

These create a sacred space no matter what the gender of the individuals concerned. It is the space of the goddess not the god. It is intimate, intuitive, emotional. It is Heart not Head. It depends on the incarnate spirit, on flesh and blood and bone. It is the space in which the mother goddess affirms the life of her children, in which we meet Sophia the creative power and wisdom of God.

I did not meet her again through textiles until many years of adult life had passed. In your teens you are divided into Science or Arts, and if you study medicine, you are Science, although the practice of it is an Art which takes years of struggle to learn. It is a life which is rewarding and creative, but not in the conventional artistic sense.

In the early 1970s I saw an embroidered picture in an exhibition in the Cardiff museum which almost certainly influenced me greatly, though I do not remember who the artist was. It showed a table set with a teacup and cakes on a plate, tilted towards the viewer, and the lower torso and hands of an old woman. It was marvellously padded and realistic, inviting you to share her world and her tea. It could not have had its effect in any other medium and I had never before realised that embroidery could be expressive, witty and sensual all at the same time. It also seemed part of the wonderful world of women's secrets which is also all of those things.

When I myself took up embroidery it was for a long time almost like a secret other life, only it became richer and fuller all the time until it burst out of its confines and took me over!

Many other textile artists have influenced me in recent years, particularly Eirian Short's "The Movil Foxes". It moved me unbearably even in a simple print. It showed me that your embroidery could also be angry and deeply unsettling. Its dark message was inextricably linked to the softness and prettiness of the stitched fur, drawing one in as a discomforted voyeur.

The railway journey with which I started this writing occurred during a time of family bereavement soon after my own retirement from work. As we drew near the station, barely recognisable after 40 odd years, I experienced a sudden longing to jump out of the train and run! I wanted to run through the streets to find my old home. My eyes filled with tears as I recognized the irrationality and impossibility of this.

I was in a Borderland, a crossing place of past and present, life and death, work and leisure, head and heart. The words and images turned and coiled in my mind like the wheel of fortune, like Inanna's descent and return ... like a mandala ... this time bound ladder ... called time ... no time at all ... no time like the present ... time traveller ... travel hopefully ... moving on ...

My eyes jerked open on the borderland between sleep and waking, to watch the birds swoop and rise by the railway track, those symbols of freedom in three-dimensional space. So many things lie buried here, waiting for me to draw them out and give them life.

The Goddess herself sleeps here, waiting,,,,
Journeys end in lovers meeting,,,,
Guarded by wings so many things
shall come to birth.
They will emerge again
Like skulls and bones and teeth and flowers
Out of the earth,
Where once the sacred Ash was burned
There will be life again within the Borderlands,
That time forgot and memory spurned.
No need for speech,
Where time stands still, with feet in clay
But we reach out to touch the day.
Under the grass the goddess sleeps,
But not too deep, and as I pass
She weeps, she weeps, alas alas

Elinor Kapp

UNLIKE THE SWAN

Unlike the swan of whom the poet wrote
That death approaching had unloosed her song,
The sorrow of your death has made me mute
And torn away the music from my tongue.

And yet, another organ seems to sound,
Whose grief-notes beat too low for human ear;
An Orpheus-gift to heal a gaping wound,
Or call a soul back from beyond despair.

When Orpheus was himself in pieces torn
His tongue swanned downwards,
singing on the waves.
The music of the soul in death is born,
And brings back beauty from the land of graves.

And so my ravaged mouth opens and sings
An echo for those beating silver wings.

LETTER TO A SON FROM A MOTHER

I am writing this letter to you, Son,
Writing it in my head as I lie here -
Under the lamp with the green duster
Tied on it, spilling light over the floor,
And the old lady in the next bed
Sighs, turns over and snores –
Because in the day, when sister lets you all
Come flooding into the ward at four o'clock
I will say nothing to you of these things.
You will come awkwardly over, your shoes
Creaking a protest to this antiseptic place,
This bustling, lively waiting room of Death,
And smile, "'Lo Mum," the book the flowers,
The talcum. bed socks, all the barricade
We build between us to shut out the words,
'This is the cancer hospital, Ward Z. Terminal.'

It is surprisingly easy to die.
I wish I could tell you about the green fields.

HOMAGE TO MY LATE HUSBAND

A strong rock. A secret fortress on a hill.
None can come near save by your will.
My waves of passion beat in a free tide
You smile, indifferent, you do not deride,
For so invulnerable the rock that I call you
That you can smile at me, and yield a few
Kind words to ease my torment.
Well, I am content,
For from my shifting base I see the way you went.

Within your topmost tower I see a beacon shine
And know your loneliness
the closest thing to mine

DEATH OF MY LOVE

Your glory of limbs
Sprawled in the mud.
Eyes deep as all time
Filming with blood.

Hair gold as the sun
Dappled with red.
How shall I mourn?
I too am dead.

My eyes have no tears,
The dead cannot weep.
The dead have no fears
And dreamless their sleep.

My death is forever
Buried with thine,
Here, where they sever
Your body from mine.

Grief heavy as stones
Heavy as lead.
Earth on your bones
Earth on my head.

I must still stay
Over the ground,
My mouth all awry
Making no sound.

Yet at the end,
When God calls all men,
It is me he will send
To find you again.

At the end of the sleep
You will open your eyes
To my kiss on your cheek
In a new paradise

PEG-TOOTHED HOLLOW-NOSED JOHN

Death was my lover and I bore a son,
I called him Hollow-nosed John.
He'd scabs on his face and peg shaped teeth
And he died before he was born.

They fed him well and they kept him dry
And I cradled his pumpkin head.
Seven times seven the days went by
Before they would call him dead.

Was it all my fault? Do you find it strange
That I cry to the gods above?
It's many of you give counterfeit change
In return for the coin of love.

The dirty old man who twitches my skirt,
The copper who leers and grins
At the teenage tart with her hips aflirt,
-I'm paying for all their sins.

Girls in the street wheeling prams piled high
With babies like fat pink buns,
Don't turn and spit as you pass me by,
You are the lucky ones.

I was born with a cross for the Holy claim,
But now that I'm going to die
I'm marked with an S in the Devil's name,
In the rotting flesh of my thigh.

For I had a son, and I called his name
Peg-toothed Hollow-nosed John.
Mine was the sorrow but yours is the shame.
He died before he was born

NOTE

PEG-TOOTHED HOLLOW-NOSED JOHN. This poem
was written in 1970, when I was 33 years old, medically
qualified and studying Psychiatry. Among the distressing
things to learn was the effect of Congenital Syphilis on a
baby or child and also on the mother. In this case she is
barely more than a child herself, shunned and blamed by
society while whatever man was responsible, as often,
remained untouched and unblamed. It is no one individual –
alas I knew quite a lot of cases – and I am angry on their
behalf and on that of the children, with signs of
Hutchinson's Syphilis; distorted facial features and peg
shaped teeth, often with only a short lifespan.

Elinor Kapp

RAIN ON BUSHES.

The writing of the mystical experience
Always turns out to be a poem,
Perhaps because the vision itself
Is the poetry of the soul,

We see how a bent and withered branch
May hold sparkling mirrors of rain.
Do not scorn banal and words
If they reflect the window to eternity.

Look at Julian though!
Her every phrase rings like a crystal ball
And holds the body like a warm robe.

NOTE

This poem was written at a conference on Julian of Norwich,
at the Hawkesyard Priory in September 1980. I had been a
devoted reader of this mystical woman since my mid-teens
at school, where I was given a book about her.

REBELLION

You have taken from me, God, my only treasure!
Like a harsh creditor who gives no time
You repossessed him. Lord, no legal measure
Can serve my turn, for you have done no crime!
He was your own creation, so am I,
Lent for a little to this world of light.

Less hard would be it for me could I cry
Loud vengeance on you. Shout into the night
Your heartless perfidy, Oh God - you thief!
A slave, even, can proclaim thus - in his heart.
But I - why God, you even made my grief,
And my rebellion is your work of art!

Then have me as you will, in grief or joy,
And I'll yield up your child, my golden boy.

Elinor Kapp

IT WAS NOT A MATTER OF AGE
BETWEEN US

It was not a matter of age between us.
I could talk better, tell you the names of things,
And do up the buttons at your neck,
But you knew more about love.
Like light on water your eyes rippled
With ever-moving emotions.

You scored my complacent surface
With grooves of urgent feeling,
Stormed me with sudden hatreds
And quick, immediate kisses.
You were unashamed as unfallen man
Of love's complete dependence.

You taught me your way of loving.
We shared an incandescent joy
In a safe, bright bubble of days.
I too was a baby and hand in hand
We ran out into the shiny world,
Laughing like children in love.

And then you ran
Out and away into a different existence,
Leaving me behind.
They said the car hit you
Because you were not very wise
And did not know how the world hurts.

You are wiser now
And older than your mother
You have eternity for birthday
And you know that the world
will always hurt the young
And turn them into something different.

I have grown older too.
I pick my way between the black pits.

Elinor Kapp

HOMAGE TO MY TEACHERS

When I was young we mocked
the Chemistry Mistress,
Because she was gentle and fat
And looked, we said, like a bus.
The young are sharp and bright
like hunting knives
And clot together in packs
Against the dark of the centuries.
In the dawn-time of my civilisation
Compassion stirred for her, and was stifled,
Lest I too be thrust from the pack.

Others we loved and raised as totems,
But secretly knew we chose other paths.
Warm salty ways of fantasy and desire,
Despising the sunlit spinster road they trod,
Manless and barren, they had no children,
We thought, in our ignorance and conceit.
Oh surely, as Job said, we were the people!
Wisdom and knowledge would perish with us!
The promise of life crowded our loins.

Now in my middle ages, so-called maturity,
Learning at last, with Blake,
to bear the beams of love,
How changed is the historical perspective!
Knowing that the best that I can hope for
On my deathbed, tomorrow, or at ninety two,
That someone will say,
"This promising piece of dust,"
I look back and see the riches poured by you
On a stone age tribe
who hardly knew how to begin,
Yet grew the centuries in a few short years.

I look back too at the secret paths
And the sunlit road, looking at last for my mother.
Now a mother myself of two small children,
And one small grave,
and a great many other people,
Who each share a piece of the maternal
Love and fury and indifference,
I begin to feel the shape of the word.
Sorrow and homage reach back and find
Sources of motherhood all through the years.

You, who did more than teach,
forgive me. I was blind.
Oh Mothers of my soul, my heart, my mind.

WRITTEN FROM THE HEART

The heart is a pump
they told us at the school of medicine
back when I was young

it has four chambers
each with its own and separate task
to circulate the blood
all eight pints or more of viscous fluid

then there's all the tubes they said
they are containers too
it would all get very messy
if that red blood were not contained!

It's only a pump they said
we boys and girls
for we were little more
eyed one another up
ignoring the lecturer
our glances boxing with gentleness and skill
touch of a hand
pressure of foot
fluttering heartbeat
a smile a proposition
expecting the answer no
it was another world then
when I was young.

It's only a pump they said
a set of boxes
keeping the body going
we knew they lied
and we contained the lie, professionally,
and held it close throughout our lives.

It's only a pump the surgeon told me
before he opened its container
and cut respectfully
into the boxes of my heart
I have been glad of that
glad that in my six hour sleeping death
my blood was still busily
going round and round
circulated by pumps outside the box
and the lung cavities were
filled and emptied by machines

my frozen heart gave up its secrets
to the surgeon's skill
then it sighed
and obediently returned to life
to everyone's relief
It's only a pump
the surgeon said
no trouble at all
we both knew he lied
and oh how grateful I am to him for that!

it was all put back into the box
sorted and tidied mended healed
restored
after all
It's only a pump the heart

except that out of it has poured
in all its redness
seventy years of dreams
exposure is complete
my heart is now open to all
and nothing will ever be the same

you can't expect somehow to return
the sighs desires conspiracies and fires
of seventy years into a box
and hope they'll circulate again discreetly
contained and hidden,
can you now? the lie's exposed
spilling its bright message everywhere . . .

No! No! hold it in and spell it out
say after me -

the **Heart** is **Only** a **Pump**

THE FEAR OF THE LORD IS
THE BEGINNING OF WISDOM.

[Proverbs 9.10]

Oh please don't come too close, or speak too clear!
It would be too much if you called to me
Out of that fiery elderberry bush.

Come on a solemn Sunday, in the Town,
Not here, not in the Wild.
I need a hiding place
Among the congregations of the good.

Call on me instead in a Cathedral close,
Where worshipers of words will hold me down
With weights of theological debate.

Angels are hovering within this little church,
stirring the rushes.
I open wide my eyes the better not to see them.

Please keep the door shut! I really can't go in.
Oh my Beloved! Don't you see?
If you should break my world apart
We might fall out.

THE CONVERSATION OF WHALES.

The conversation of whales
Is slow and deep and strange.
Eerie blowholes of nouns, and
Mournful adjectives, spilling away
Endlessly through the oceans,
A haunting grammar of sounds,
Green silences, and punctuations
Of strange long beats. Glassy seas
And oceans rolling with tides,
Ship sounds, bell sounds,
Smack of waves and fins, go
Echoing over old hulls of hulks,
And through blue-patterned dunes,
Where whales sway and turn
Stirring the cumuli of sand.
Endless questioning spume-filled calls
Stretch through the sea miles
To interrogate the ocean.

If you want to follow the whales,
No – even more – to converse,
You must enter the sea. Dare
The treacherous waves pulling
You down. You must swim
Close to the whales, come to
That last terrified inch, where
The whale's skin takes you in
Its razor embrace, risking
The careless murder of the tail.
Close, closer still, meeting at last
The alien enquiry of the eye.
Even then, even more, you must
Submerge. Cease to breathe
Through natural orifices. Grow to be
Large as Leviathan. Every cell
Spaced out like a coral reef;
Thoughts deep as the tides
Slowly surging and receding.

Tide- race of juices, salty, strong,
Pour in torrents of blood
Into your cathedral heart,
Through great vessels, sounding
Organ notes. Booming tunes
Echo in your cave of ribs,
Where the bones are like ships.
Every pulse as long as a beach
And high as a curling wave.

Oh but it would be worth it!
Worth risking the pull and suck
Of the sea as you returned –
But would you return; if so
Would you remember?

Oh what if
Nothing could be recalled?
If you had nothing to share?
Mute as a mermaid! Even so,
Even so, it surely would be worth
Each stolen heart beat,
To have shared for a while
In the long green life of the ocean tides,
And the conversation of whales.

NOTE
I wrote this poem in 1992 while sitting with my much-loved
husband in his final weeks. Later on I read it many times at
poetry events, with a soft background of whale sounds,
without saying anything about the origin of the poem. Every
single time at least two people would come up to me
privately afterwards, saying that it reminded them of the
death of someone they loved, often with tears.

WHEN I WAS JUST FIFTEEN

When I was just fifteen I had a crush
On all romantic poets, turn by turn;
But oh, John Keats, you were my one true love.

For you the roses bloomed upon my bush,
I'd have rejoiced for you to feel them burn.
You loved elsewhere, elsewhile,
not this sweet dove.

There on your hands the crimson telltale blush
Of Death's red roses, as your fate you learn.
Atropos cut your thread, from realms above.

Love given young sets up a template true.
I'll never love a lesser man than you.

NOTE

This poem was written in 2018. The memory is accurate but
I could not have written it in 1952 when I was fifteen years
old.

STONE FRIEND

"Shall I be your friend?" said the Stone.
"Your Stone friend?
"Did I choose you, or did you choose me
Stone Friend," he asked her.
He sat with her in his hand,
slept with her by his pillow,
carried her all day.

As she rested against his ear,
mineral on shell-flesh,
He heard her whisper in his dreams,
"I was once part of a great mountain
of stone," she said.
"How was it?" he asked her.
"It was good, good, good," said his Stone Friend.

In his dreams he heard his Stone Friend chanting,
"My mountain lasted a million, million,
million years,

It froze and thawed, froze and thawed.
Water crept into spaces, ice stretched,
ice melted, cracks grew,
Water crept into spaces, ice stretched,
ice melted, cracks grew,
Water crept into spaces, ice stretched,
ice melted, cracks grew.

Suddenly, the mountain split.
We thundered down the plain,
As many rocks as there are stars in the sky."

"How was it?" he asked her.
"It was good, good, good," said his Stone Friend,
In his half-sleep he felt the rush of water
over a bed of rocks,

Or was it bodies, rolling, melting, rotting –
pebbles and bones rolling,
rolling down to the great sea?

He dreamed again,
and heard his Stone Friend say,
"I was ground down by water,
smashed against rocks,
jostling and crushing and scraping till I
became as I am now."
"How was it?" he asked his Stone Friend,
"It was good, good, good," she said.

"For many ages I was part of a stone cairn,"
she said.
"We guarded a King.
Men came and went,
came and went,
came and went,
Then the water returned and swept it all away."
"How was that?" he asked.
"It was good, good, good," said his Stone Friend.

He told his Stone Friend,
"I took you from a basket once,
Now I am leaving, where shall I put you?"
"You can put me in a basket, or in the earth,
or in the water," said his Stone Friend.
"I'm going to miss you.
Doesn't it matter to you?" he asked,

Are you going to miss me?" he said
"Yes, I will miss you," said his Stone Friend,
"But I will miss you because I had you,
and it is good, good, good, good, good!"

Elinor Kapp

EPITAPH FOR AN ANOREXIC GIRL
{written 1999}

This girl never blossomed, never bore fruit.
Her life was broken by secret battles
In a war no one ever declared.

She fought determinedly through fat and thin,
No one gave her an alternative.
      There is no ceasefire.
           no armistice.
           no medal
           no honourable discharge
           no peace in our time
      For this bone-thin army of girls,
To which she never knew she was conscripted.

This girl thought that she alone had heard
The call-up trumpet thrilling in her gut.
She wore the pared down uniform with pride.

When at the end she found herself alone
      in a muddy foxhole
      in no-man's land
      blindfolded
      deafened
      and gagged,
      She fired randomly at friend and foe,
And rescue came too late.

NOTE

I would like to note here, that young girls with Anorexia Nervosa were a large part of our work. It is a very serious condition, with a frightening mortality rate unless recognised, taken seriously and treated with great care and understanding. It occurs increasingly in boys too.

Our team in this was led by our long-term Senior Sister, Joy Jones, who worked for many years to understand and treat the condition, becoming a recognised authority on it and passing on her knowledge. May I be indulged if I end here by putting in a poem that I wrote as a sort of tribute to all these girls, struggling with eating disorders, particularly those we could not save?

Elinor Kapp

THE PRINCESS AND THE PLOUGHBOY

Late one night as the Princess lay
All alone in the castle keep,
Where ivy crumbles the walls away
And the friendly mice patter and peep,

A light wind came through the broken glass,
And the beasts on the hangings, heavy and worn,
Stirred and danced as the breeze blew past,
And over the sill leapt a unicorn.

With his golden mane and his silver pelt
A glory fell on the threadbare room,
The tapestry horses swayed and knelt,
Heraldic lions stepped back in the gloom.

The mice cried warnings, cold with fright,
But onto his back the Princess sprang,
And over the sill like a wand of light
He bore her away; and the Princess sang

For joy of her flight, and the coming day,
And the leagues rushed by under silent hooves,
Till far beneath, in the twilight grey
She thought she could see the village roofs.

Then she cried out loud at a distant dream
As they circled and swooped to the forest floor
And as she alighted she saw a gleam
Of light flowing out from a cottage door.

A ploughman's cottage, small and cozy,
And there asleep in an easy chair
The ploughboy sprawled, his cheeks were rosy,
The firelight shone on his ginger hair.

In the coppery glow there a ginger cat
Slept on the rug, lazy as Lob,
Paws under tummy, buttery fat,
And a kettle sputtered and sang on the hob.

The Princess clapped her hands in delight
And ran to the hearth to make the tea.
The ploughboy knelt at her feet and cried
Humbly, Princess, will you marry me?"

THE FETCH

Be ready for me, little sister!
I am your grey wolf lover.
I will sit down at your hearth
And lay my cold fingers on your heart.

Sometimes my beak will peck you lovingly.
You will hardly feel the blood draining away.
Sometimes I will squat on your face,
My dusty feathers stopping your breath
With long forgotten mould.

And I will never, never leave you,
My monkey arms winding your neck,
My breath on your cheek, smelling of dung.
Be ready for me, little sister! Be ready!

CONFERENCE

I met a man at a conference
And flirted with him in the bar.
He'd just come back from Romania
Where he met Ceauşescu's niece.
"She had two small puncture marks
 on her neck," he said.
Points to his jugular, rolling his eyes.

We flirted, talked of Vampires,
Talked some more – Roman pottery,
Welsh stone heads that tell the future.
Macsen Wledig and the Mabinogion.
We flirted some more, parted for the night.

In my sparse student room
Alone at the top of the tower block,
I took a calculated risk
And left the window open.
The Vampire never came.

GWYDION WAKES THE BIRCH TREE

Stone down solid deep deep deep sleep sleep sleep
Earth down suck slurp, fountain up, breathe out.
Worms slide, wingy-things hum, buzz, swirl,
Sun drops flirt and finger, smile,
smooth and stroke.
Rain shine tickles and teases
titillates down each twig.

Master of magic, Gwydion calls my name —
Beth I am; Birch. Root and branch I roar
With the anguish of gods, of becoming myself.
My roots go so deep the tearing up feels as if
It will kill me. Filled with Gwydion's purpose,
Not my own, late I am coming. My twigs,
Once made to drive out evil and madness, bristle.
My sweetness, once used to heal and to nourish,
Is a burning. I am filled with so deadly a rage
Nothing can hold me, nothing withstand me.
I am not in the image of a loving god,
I am swordrage bloodrant and firecurse
I am Death.

HUW: GORSEINON HOSPITAL 1943

Did you die,
Or did they just take you away
To another ward?
Boy in the next bed,
Plaster legs high on a gallows
Where your small body hung.
You smiled at me
With all your seven years,
And I, a year younger,
Fell in love with you, there and then and
Always and forever.
Huw, Huw, Huw: the cooing of a dove.
For hours we talked about the Fairy Folk
I knew they were a story,
You did not. Shy, hospital-bound child,
Older and younger than your years.
Not for the world
Would I have disillusioned you.
I would have held your ears
In my child-small hands.
I would have given all I had
To save you from that truth.
Neither, for all the world
Would I have let you go.
Did the Fairy Folk take you?
Did you die?
Or did they just take you away
To another ward?

SPRING IN THE CIVIC CENTRE

The Mayor considered that the gardens ought
To have a share in Spring.
Tulips would be respectable, he thought,
Quiet, and quite the thing.

"Obedient tulips stand in rows," he said,
"And never make a mess,
But to make sure, we'll still fence off the bed."
The councillors said "Yes."

But oh, if they had only known the truth!
The Spring can't be confined.
Those wild and dangerous tulips, like our youth,
Subvert the civic mind.

The typists, all seduced from sober ways,
Remove their woolly vests,
While golden waves of flowers fall in spray
Around their naked breasts.

The treasurer cries "How erroneous!
The scheme has fallen flat.
Next year I say, stick to begonias,
And plastic ones at that!"

The stripy tulip-tigers roar, and try
To reach with yellow paws
And swipe the ankles of the passers-by,
Gnashing their crimson jaws.

Pubescent schoolgirls walk in twosomes near,
Still thinking of their sums.
Those saucy orange tulips wink and leer,
And try to pinch their bums.

Tell all the filing clerks to stay away –
Some things cannot be filed.
With sex and aggro in the park today,
The Spring is really wild!

Elinor Kapp

MARKET GARDEN

Dry tears of leaving rutted down my face.
I stopped my car, not knowing where I was,
by a farm shop, one sunshine, leaf-drop day.

Three tiny dogs barked, wagging their tails,
eyes bright with love. Then they lay down.
I was accepted, silent tears and all.

A boy, sorting shallots, smiled, ducked his head.
The farmer briskly left off digging veg,
to make a cup of tea in the empty caff.

I bought leeks fresh with earth, potatoes,
jams, jars and jellies, the boy's shallots,
all ridiculously cheap; he gave the tea for free!

Air moved, sun shone, dogs slept, I left.
I fried the shallots, watching Coronation Street,
And ate the potatoes mashed, with milk and salt.

Their other name is 'Apples of the earth,'
And I recalled the triple-headed dog
who guarded them.

A woman, in another Garden, scrumped one once,
but mine were fairly bought, and paid in tears
dropped from the heart, and copper cash –
although it was ridiculously cheap.

Earth apples bought by tears, or gold, or blood,
become the Golden Apples of the Sun.
I never tasted food so good before.

That Garden where I stopped – I know its name.
I know the Gardener who walked with me.
And the tea was given free.

Elinor Kapp

LULLABY FOR THE MOTHER
OF A DEAD CHILD

Oh cradle the child as if he were sleeping.
Lullaby mother, and hushed be your weeping.
The tears are not his, nor the pain and the sorrow,
For he is awake in a golden tomorrow.

It is you who are sent to a darkness unending.
Whipped for no fault, you lie, uncomprehending
Oh desolate child, you must wait for the dawning,
But your son is awake
on a bright summer morning.

Strong hands hold him up and he
chuckles with laughter,
Grasping at stars and the Angels laugh, after.
Then, petted and kissed,
from their knees he is springing
To search the green fields
where the children are singing.

LANDSCAPE

There is a fruitful land wherein I dwell,
My home is here, within a garden fair.
The house is small, but suits me very well.
Come in, converse. I'll find fine fruit to share.

Come, taste my flowers, listen to my birds,
Enjoy my sunshine. Yours not to see the earth,
The cesspit, hard worked compost,
dung and turds,
That bring my lavish roses into birth

The night bird gives a tortured cry of warning,
As darkness over land and garden falls,
And trees grow to the light, to touch the morning.
This is the fruitful land which in me dwells

SIMPLICITY

When I came home and parked the car today
God said to me, "Please come for a walk,
down by the river. Come with Me!"
I thought – I want my tea, a little sleep,
a mindless program on the telly. But God was
teasing me, as if I was a child. He said,
"I want to show you something. What if I say,
"pretty please with a cherry on?" So I went.
We walked through the park and to the river,
in the teatime, glowtime, of the autumn sun.

There I saw the white dancer, the Birch Tree,
leaning breathless towards her Linden lover.
His trunk was mossed with green. Sunshine,
reflected from her leaves, transmuted all
to peacock and to gold. The trefoil ivy twined
to join them in a heart to heart embrace.
They demonstrate the Alchemist's retort
'Green is for Go, the way is clear!'
Heaven shines before me by the water.

I longed to share it.
When a man passed by, I said,
"Look, isn't the river pretty in the autumn sun!"
He answered in a foreign accent, quite confused,
then laughed and smiled and thanked me nicely.
The next man, wheeling his bike,
Was typically embarrassed, didn't say a thing,
but as he moved away he called back to me,
"I love coming out, this time of year,
seeing the sun on the leaves!"
and I called "Thanks!"

We are three points on the ivy leaf,
linked by water,
drawn up from the river, through the roots.
I am a birch leaf, I am the moss,
the bank, the sky.
I am the passing strangers, and they my lovers.
I am Heaven itself, and Heaven is me
here by the water, by the river, in the gold.

Then God said, "You can go home now."
So I went home to have my tea.
I slept on the sofa, while God watched my dreams.
He held my hand and said,
"Thank you, my Beloved."

SPRING SONG

I asked for the Spring to caress you
And clothe you in daffodils bright,
But Winter insisted he dress you
In icicles silver and white.

Spring said, better not to distress you
And quietly left in the night.
Leaving only the moonshine to bless you,
In the ghost of a snowdrop's light.

SO MANY VARIED MASKS

A masked and mincing Actor-man
Came through the wall with painted fan.
I knew him instantly, "It's Death.
He's come to fan away your breath,"
I cried. "He says you can't refuse
To dance with him in scarlet shoes.
Look – there he is beside your bed!"

"Tell him to go away," you said,
And smiled at me, but well we knew
Once death has got you in his view
He won't give up. In different guise
He'll come and catch you by surprise.

He wore so many varied masks
That sometimes in my household tasks
I'd meet him, and with fingers sly
He'd grope my heart in passing by.

You never saw him, but you knew
That raven wings about you flew,
Sent by his hand, and you would say,
"Don't worry love, we'll keep at bay
The sly old rogue as best we can,"
And I would see the Actor-man
Change to a mask of different style,
And so concede defeat awhile.

Oh he had many, many ways
To make his presence known those days!
Sometimes I'd find him by your chair,
Or reaching out to touch your hair.
Later he'd dress in skull and bones,
A childhood bogey, making groans,
Or else I'd only sense him near,
With just a feather-hint of fear.
A rattle, as of night-birds' claws,
Or warm wet opening of jaws,
An adder's hiss, a jackal's bark,
A furry feeling in the dark.

"You hardly call your soul your own
With him around," you'd sometimes moan
As he came mincing up the stair.
At last we'd meet him everywhere,
With no escape. Yet at the end
We welcomed him, and called him Friend,
And instantly the mask was gone
And only light within him shone.

A FATHER'S PRIDE

I rest my arms against the window-rod.
The January sun
Small fiery ball, naked against the mist
Leans on my cheek.

Her labour done,
My wife lies resting, quiet, triumphant, meek,
She smells of meadow-sweet, sunkissed.
Crooked in her gentle arm
The little one
Protests no more, sucking a crimpled fist.

"For out of Egypt have I called my son!"
I feel like God!

NOTE
This is another example of a poem written empathetically to
explore the emotions of other people. I wrote it in 1967 when
a friend's wife gave birth and I was privileged to be there.

BATTLE ABBEY

Did Harold stand upon this place,
Shielding his eyes like me,
As Hastings-ward he turned his face
To look toward the sea?

And did he see through wind-forced tears
Grim ranks of iron shields,
Where sheep had grazed a thousand years
Upon these Sussex Fields?

Tall trees about this place are ranged,
Peace is returned for strife,
Nine hundred times their leaves have changed,
Life, death, and back to life.

No pilgrim struggles to this place,
The monks have long since gone,
Only the tourists try and trace
Where England's heroes shone.

Unlike the Swan

Pretending still I raise my eyes
To share the seagulls' wheel,
I change their calls to battle cries
And clash of steel on steel.

The sun is warm. Over his earth
The shadows interlace.
I dream a while of death and birth
With tears upon my face.

I see no ghost, no sound he hears.
The sheep are grazing still,
As they have grazed 2000 years
Upon this Sussex hill

YORBOROUGH SOMEDAY

The stone walls carry lines of sight
Where Yourber rears against the light,
Then bring the eye back down the hill.
Stones, tumbled from the candle mill
Among the ash roots in the stream,
Afford a place to sit and dream
With meadowsweet and harebells near.
Someday I'll sit there. Far but clear,
Blown on the wind I'll hear your voice.
"Rejoice my dearest dear, rejoice."

MESSAGES FROM A SMALL PRIVATE WAR

1 TWELVE POINT TURN

In Bosnia you do a twelve-point turn,
Because they mine the road edges.
Death is a drastic way to fail your driving test.

In love, on the other hand,
you haul the wheel around
Any old way,
Because the worst you will get is –
        Stuck
           Toppled over
              Surprised from in front
                Astonished from behind
              Confused
                humiliated,
                  and adored.

MESSAGES FROM A SMALL PRIVATE WAR

2 COMBAT MANUAL FOR LOVERS.

SUBSECTION Four B.
How to get through a minefield.

1. Sometimes the only way to keep the peace
is to have a big bang

2. If you are very careful
you can set off small controlled explosions.

3. Run in a zigzag. If blown up,
lie down and think of England.

4. A good bang can be more fun for the spectators
than for the couple.

5. No matter where lovers lie down
they always wake up in a minefield

6. Proper Reconnaissance beforehand
is an absolute necessity.

MESSAGES FROM A SMALL PRIVATE WAR

3 FIELD HOSPITAL

Whenever I fall in love,
Which is, to exaggerate, once or twice a week,
I put up barricades, earthworks, barbed wire,
And gun emplacements. What's the use?
As soon as they're in place
I walk right round them.
I look at my Army Manual. It says clearly
On page one, Instruction one, stroke A,

"DON'T DANCE ON THE EDGES OF MINEFIELDS"

But it's so beautiful there, so special,
The poppies are scarlet, and crumpled
like rose petals,
Promising the sweetest oblivion.

I wake in the field hospital, crying,
With the other war-wounded fools.
Then I get up, and limp around a bit,
Bragging about my scars.

BE VERY, VERY CAREFUL, MY DEAR!

Be mindful of the tiger
who nightly prowls the town,
You must turn the lights up quickly,
and pull the shutters down.
Protect your house securely,
as tightly as a box,
With iron bars and chains around,
cos tigers can't pick locks.

Although it means you'll never see
the beauty of the night,
It's safety first, don't take a chance,
nor ever risk a fright.
Put guards around your premises
and padlock up your soul,
And never let the tiger in,
or you'll be swallowed whole.

Just when you think it's all secure,
there's treachery within.
Someone's left a tiny crack,
and quickly as a sin
A lithe and sexy shadow-shape
is sliding through the gate,
You look into those amber eyes
and know that it's too late.

THE MODRON AND THE MABON

"And Modron gave birth to Mabon, who on the third day was taken from between his mother and the wall."

We are your children, Modron,
but have held you cheap,
Mined riches from your heart, defiled your hall,
Poisoned the holy wells
mocking the tears you weep.
Lost is the love that should combine us all,
So now when darkness falls we are afraid to sleep.
Yet in the end each one will hear your call,
Eternal Mother, and for each of us you'll keep
A space between your body and the wall.

NOTE

The opening sentence is from the historic Welsh poem, the Mabinogion. The Modron simply signifies 'the Mother' and the Mabon, 'the Son, or Boy. Later in the book he is spoken of as having been imprisoned in a tower in a lake near [present day] Gloucester since before recorded time, and his rescue involves the protagonists in numerous heroic tasks, but there is no explanation.

There is another use of 'the stolen baby' motif in the Mabinogion, and it is quite common in myth and folklore. Hugh Lupton and Eric Maddern suggest that here it refers to some very ancient religious theme and ritual relating to the early goddess culture. Insignificant as the fragment seems they believe it is probably the core and secret meaning underlying the whole Mabinigion cycle.

I thought long about the significance of the particular words, and feel sure that they are intended to show that the child could only have been taken by supernatural means and not a human enemy.

GRACE

I came to the meeting place in the dark wood,
I fell ahead, my knees and hands grasped soil,
and said, "This is beyond me.
Only God can Forgive."
God hung forward from His tree and groaned.

I leaned deeper into the night's darkness
and said "Only I can forgive." and I groaned.
Forgiveness rolled through the wood like thunder,
God talking to God.

NOTE
This poem was written on June 26th 2016 at a meditation
weekend at Llansor Mill.

TWENTYONE TUDOR LADIES

Twelve Tudor Ladies
are Sipping Sirops on the Terrace.
Munching Morsels of Marchpane, they Sigh,
    and Eye the Tudor Gallants
    Parading in the Maze.
As they Gaze they long to be Pursued
    and Persuaded to a Pavane
    or to a Galliard, two by two.
But the Astute Gallants
set a more Subtle Snare
Pretend not to Perceive them!
    Feigned Indifference a more sure Pursuit.
    by this Conceit fanning their Fancies
    Fire to further heat.

Six Ladies, very neat
are Sewing Silently on the Lawn.
Garments gilded with Galloon
are graced with Gillyflowers –
    Burlesqued Festoons, fooling the Bees,
    who murmur their Summer Tunes
    to Marigolds beside the Pool.
Ivory Oversleeves of softest Lawn
    swirled by the Breeze
    uncover curling Stems
    and Blackworked Leaves.

They Spangle and Speckle and Seed with Knots,
    Not sowing of Plots
but the Silken stuff
where their Knot Garden is Sewn.

Here is shown the Pleasing prospect of an Arbour.
A Tranquil Harbour where three Ladies,
all alone, partake
    of Carraway Cake, Comfits
    and Candied Cherries.
Tendrils and Berries of the Trellised Vine
    Quaintly combine with Peach,
    each with each Plait, Pleach and Twine,
Marvellously mimicking the Filigree Laces
    framing their Faces.
Creating their own Delights
of the Needle's Devising,
    Pricking Patterns in Parchment,
    surprising Designs of Clover and Columbine –
The Ladies concentrate Dutifully.

Dulcimer, Flute, mellifluous Viola da Gamba are
playing Beautifully,
    by Beckoning Beds made up
    with Sheets of Heartsease, sure to please,
    Pillows of Pinks, covers of Chamomile,
    and Damask Roses for Valance.
Those Ladies on the Terrace
are Peeping Privily at the Gallants,
    Ogling and making Artful Designs on them.
But though the Ladies on the Lawn
and under the Arbour
    keep their Eyes down,
All Twentyone of them drown
in Desires for Amorous Dalliance.

Elinor Kapp

PHILOMELA SINGS

I am a bird,
I sing while others sleep, and am not heard.
My voice proclaims
A territorial warning but no names,
And no one heeds.
My song is angry, telling of such deeds
That if you heard
You'd stop your ears, not listen to a word.

The cadence floats
Over the shadowed garden, sending notes
Pregnant with doom
To where my sister, bowed above her loom
Endlessly grieves,
And pieces out her story as she weaves.

It can be read,
But who will care enough to trace the thread?
Or will they cry,
"You surely have embroidered it, you lie"
For mine are songs
That will disturb complacency with wrongs,
And foul your ears.

The husband's monstrous shadow fumbles, peers,
A stifled cry,
An arm thrown up then sinking with a sigh'
The blood's bright flow
Is all inside. There's nothing much to show.

I am the Nightingale, whose song is sung
For every woman who has lost her tongue

*

NOTE

The Greek legend of the two sisters, Procne and Philomela,
and the murderous husband is such a dark and tragic tale
that I do not want to speak of it! I was fascinated by the way
that Philomela communicated through weaving the story
into a blanket, when I was collecting textile stories!

I wrote a brief verse in my 1968 diary, then it later inspired
the longer poem –

"When they fall silent into slumber
and all the songs of love are sung
and the music of lute and viol is gone.
Then the Minstrels will sing
for the dumb Nightingale
with her outrooted tongue."

Elinor Kapp

THE SILVER THIMBLE

{for Hymie and his sister,
who shared the story with me}

"Look!" holding out his hand to her he cries,
"I have the sea!"
Within the silver circle dolphins rise,
Ships dance, and singing in the depths he finds

A mermaid where the rainbow-serpent winds
Around him. Elder sister comes to see,
"Of course you haven't! Give that back to me
You silly boy!"

Ships sink with all their hands.
The mermaid dies.
The tide goes out, and in his chastened eyes
Reflections of the beach are grey and cold.
The chalice falls.

Such pain of contradiction! Who can hold
Having and not-having in a silver bowl?
Who knows how many times the years must roll
Till the tide turns.

CONTAINERS FOR THE SOUL

My artist friend, Laurie,
keeps his soul in a tube of paint.
I worry some day he'll forget,
squeeze it onto his palette,
and paint it into a picture.
[but I guess that happens all the time]

Tony's soul sets sail in a little boat
through the valleys of Wales.
Fanned in the breeze
by the one-winged angel,
the ship of fools sails on, on, and on.
Past pub and chapel, terrace and tower;
full of contradictions and fantasies,
flowering, flowing and fine as the artist himself

Norman has a definite opinion
of where he'll keep his soul.
It's his silver vase from Norway,
full of old associations; its spare pure lines
combining structure and imagination,
just like his paintings.

It takes Mike a long time
to decide where to keep his soul.
He gives it serious consideration
for so long I give up and go.
He catches me in the car park.
"A wine glass", says Mike.

In a kaleidoscope like the ones
her father made her as a child
Kaye keeps her soul. It rests by the window
so we can share the jewelled light
sent through it by the sun.
Broken bits of soul can be so beautiful!

Lata has decided to keep her soul
in the ornamental clock made from an ostrich egg,
given by a friend, kept on the TV
in her sitting room.
"What if someone breaks it?" I cry.
"When it breaks, I pop off," she says serenely,
"but till then you can all sit and admire it!"

My daughter keeps her soul
in a butter dish in the fridge.
That's cool!

Marc says he keeps his soul
in his wife's bra. Not in the drawer either.
He says it likes lots of mothering.
I don't know if he asked her first,
but I don't suppose she minds.

Maybe it was a mistake
to ask a philosopher,
chance met at a conference,
where he would keep his soul.
"I would keep it both within
and around me," he said,
"because that is where it should be".

And after all that
where do I keep my soul?
Oh! If I could just remember that
I would go and find it.
I would look after it much better next time—
Honestly I would. I promise.

IN THE BORDERLANDS

In the Borderlands
Sometimes thieves come in the night
and carry off the sheep.
You wake, grieving,
to find more of your lambs have gone.

In the Borderlands
Unstitched wounds of mine shafts
open the turf. Abandoned casualties
Of a struggle to stay warm
and fed in harder times.

In the Borderlands
Bones of a thousand saints rise from the ground
smiling at the sky
With speedwell blue eyes.
The chapels are always full,
but only with sheep.

In the Borderlands
Occasionally the rainbow
has some new colours in it
no one has named before
 and the sun rises with a blue ring in shades
of pewter and rose.

In the Borderlands
I wait by the window each night but
my lover passes by along the corpse way.
He carries my heart carefully
in a glass to the river crossing.

In the Borderlands
The thin Welsh rain changes everything
to a soft green mist.
Out of the mouths of mine shafts
and the bones of saints come powerful songs.

TALK ME DOWN

A young man taking his first flight
Despairing made a mayday call,
Trying in haste to get it right,
"My pilot's dead. My plane will fall
Helplessly spinning on the town.
 Someone, anyone, talk me down!"

I know the feeling. As I lie
Beside you in our marriage bed,
Sharing your breathing as you die
And trapped within our love, I'm led
Too high above the living town,
Soon to be left with no way down.

Caught in an angel world of glass
Out of control I take my flight.
Watching the burning planets pass,
I cannot breathe this silver light.
Give me the human air of town -
Oh someone come and talk me down!

And what of her, the pilot's wife?
Widowhood written in the sky
Before she knew he'd lost his life.
She had no chance to say goodbye.
So often in the busy town
It happens. Someone, talk her down!

The young man lived. His may-day call
Was answered by another man,
Who talked him down. Surely we all
Can learn from this God's greater plan
To link us citizens of town
In brotherhood that talks us down?

It's not so simple! Though we try
We often find one fatal flaw;
We've let our inner pilot die
And substituted rule of law,
And voices clamour from the town
To criticise, not talk us down.

In pride too near the light we fly,
Icarus-like we risk the loss,
Yet Jesus too was heard to cry
When lifted up upon the cross
At Golgotha, outside the town,
"Oh Father help me, talk me down!"

The Icon Christ is in my heart,
The crucifixion in your bones,
And as we two are torn apart
I hear mankind's beseeching tones
Crying from all the busy town -
"Oh save us, heal us, talk us down!"

Love is the only true belief,
The purpose for which Jesus died,
So that in death, and in our grief,
We find our souls prised open wide
To reconcile both sky and town
And let Christ in, to talk us down.

NOTE
This is another poem which evolved after my long vigil
while my husband was dying. It was a real event, unfolding
on radio as it was taking place. A completely inexperienced
young man was in the air with an experienced pilot, who
had a heart attack and died – leaving the young man in a
terrible position, but to be talked down, successfully, from
Cardiff airport.

HAIKU
{Also known as Cameo Verses}

FOR HIROKO

A Japanese girl
plays a Welsh air on her koto.
Such harmony!

BY A SICKBED

In the highest hills
where the air is like glass
each indrawn breath draws blood.

The air is thin.
Rocks slip
on either side space falls away to nothing.

ABERFAN

We, guilty, slept through it all.
Rain fell. Black tip fell.
Greed, crushing childhood.

This place is sacred,
leave them now to flowers.
Keep silent your own grief.

RED KITES

Dawn sun lifts the red kites,
turns them to and fro
writing them on the sky.

Snatch the wind you brave red birds.
Fly south!
Cover the black valleys with your wings.

FRIENDSHIP

The being of one
touches the becoming of another
in a never ending spider web of ties

A friend shares his grief.
He weeps.
Love sits between us, holds our hands.

ON THE BEACH

Look! Where she danced
in pale seafoam
A mermaid's purse lies on the sand.

Iridescent flowers of the sea
dissolving
sparkle in the sun

Through green glass
and torn sea lace
we glimpse King Neptune's richest palaces.

The waves sidle up to the rocks
Smack! Pull! Push!
The doors never open.

Cool scented stone,
damp moss,
water gushes suddenly up from great depths

DEUTERONOMY Chapter 26
"My father was a wandering Aramaic."

"Oh lonely prophet, you wandering man,
Say where are you going today?"
"To Chili, Iraq and Afghanistan
And places along the way."

"Your face is sad as you endlessly roam
And your body is spattered with blood,"
"They shelled my village and burnt my home
And the children are crying for food."

"I pity you so you are gentle and good,
Let me bind up the wounds in your hands."
"No no little sister, the outflowing blood
Will make blossom these desert sands."

"Oh wanderer stop! Let me make you my own.
Stay here like a bird in its nest."
"The wood from this cross is to build up a town,
Till it's finished I cannot find rest."

"Then let me come with you, my own, my dear,
If you go I will die of the loss"
"Then come little sister, but understand clear
 you must help me to carry this cross.

We will go by the paths
that are small and straight,
 Through desert and thorn and blood.
 Your mouth will parch and your heart will ache
 And your feet leave a trail of blood."

"My heart almost fails! Yet in spite of the cost
Still will I pledge you my vows."
"Then come my bride I will bring you at last
 To the joy of my father's house."

CIRCLE DANCE

Oh most beloved, dearest, my lover,
We came to your door by your own invitation.
In the hall we caught sight of you,
Then you were gone, teasing, hiding, laughing.
A game of hide and seek, where all are winners.

We circled you in the dance,
We were nourished at your table,
We tasted the joys of talking, heart to heart,
We drank the silence, served by angels,
We slept well, we slept ill,
but always in your arms.
We caught sight of you in the words of poets
Many hundred years dead, but holding us close.

Then at last the seventh circle brought us
No more words.
Joy, joy, joy in the beloved.

THE LABYRINTH

Enter the maze if you dare,
But do dare, for it is not a puzzle maze
To confine you, to leave you
Caught in thorns on a wild path.
Trust that first glimpse you had,
Sly-angled through the cross,
And it is love.

Trust love, as you are led outer and outer,
Further and further, lonely and sometimes afraid.
Trust. Go on. Hold out your hand.
The circles come smaller, calling you in,
Backwards and forwards,
Scent lavender and wormwood, heavy with loving.
Here is the centre. Here is silence.

THE SEARCH FOR THE LOST HARP
Based on a story in the Kalevala.

{Note: Vainamoinen is roughly pronounced Vine-ar-moy-nun}

Old Vainamoinen has lost his harp
And has set out on a long search.

It was caught by the ocean, drowned in the sea,
And music has gone from the earth.

"I'm old Vainamoinen, the oldest of men,
Immortal and steadfast, and everyone's friend.

My harp is gone. The waters and foam
Have taken it down to the halls of stone.

My harp is taken, alas and alack,
And never again will I get it back.

My harp is lost and I am alone,
It is tumbled and tossed in the white sea foam.

Under the waves the fishes play,
And my harp sings alone for-ever-a-day.

My harp is gone, my harp is gone.

I'm old Vainamoinen, the oldest of men,
Immortal and steadfast and everyone's friend.

My name means 'Still waters',
still waters run deep,
From the depths of the world to the heights
I can creep.

I am the point where the ebb meets the flow.
And everything pauses till I let it go.

I am the breath which is no breath at all,
Where outbreath meets inbreath
and stillness is all.

I am the guardian of all things watery,
Seas and oceans and singing and poetry,
Semen and urine and waters of birth,
And all of the rivers that flow on the earth,
Juices of fruits and juice of the vine,
Torrents and snowstorms, all these are mine.

"Make me a rake
With nice little teeth,
I'll break out the sea
And whatever's beneath,

I've tidied up the sea,
And straightened out the sand,
But my dear little harp
Still hasn't come to hand."

The old man walks home ever so glum,
His hat all askew and his jacket undone,
When all of a sudden a Birch-tree he sees,
Standing away from the rest of the trees,
"Oh beautiful Birch-tree, you must be so glad,
Standing around giving creatures your shade,
While about you all day admirers are flocking."

But the Birch-tree replies,
"You have got to be joking!
People break off my branches to sit in my lap,
They strip off my plumage and drink up my sap.
In summer I burn and in winter I freeze,
I am the saddest of all of the trees!"

The old man caressed her bark and said,
"Oh Birch-tree you beautiful thing,
 Just trust yourself to my strong brown hands,
 And I promise I'll make you sing."

 The birch tree danced, and her leaves unfurled,
"Oh Sir, to you I will cling,
 For more than anything in the world
I want someone to make me sing!"

Old Vainamoinen jigs up and down.
And he plays on his new-made harp –

"So come everybody, get round in a ring!
Throw up your arms and start to sing!
Dance till you drop, then dance some more,
And stamp your feet like drums on the floor.

Dance till the windows rattle and shake,
Dance and sing till the rafters break!
Dance in a roundel, dance in a square,
Dance round the hearth-tree and everywhere!

Sing for your child, and your father and mother,
Sing with your enemy, sing with your brother!
Celebrate bone and flesh and breath,
Celebrate life, and celebrate death!

Sing so the fire can dance in the hearth,
Sing so the oceans can dance with the earth,
Sing to bring peace, and dance out strife,
And dance and sing the creation of life!"

So everyone danced and everyone sang,
All day from dawn till dark,
While old Vainamoinen jigged up and down
And played on his lovely harp.

Elinor Kapp

LOVEBITES

INTRODUCTION

You might want to ask, is that 'Love Bites' as in
the little red marks inflicted by amorous lovers on
each other's' skin? Or 'bites', as a verb to describe
the mordant quality of sensual relationships?
Your choice.

The human tongue only distinguishes four basic
flavours in food, and love must be the same. It can
be Sweet (oh how sweet!) and it can certainly be
Salty. It can go Sour, and it may even be Bitter. I
would like to think that these verses have a bit of
a bite, both sweet and salty, occasionally a touch
sour, but never, ever, bitter. I'm grateful for all
the encounters celebrated here.

Just to endorse that, I've included a couple of
recipes, especially for those who can't afford a diet
of oysters and champagne and other sexy fare.
Anyway, I find laughter is the best aphrodisiac.

CHOCOLATE BISCUIT CAKE

Girls, you must have a stash of chocolate somewhere that you would sacrifice for some gorgeous man. No? You'll just have to buy some more, then.

Break up as much chocolate as you can spare, preferably dark, with an equal weight of butter. Close your eyes and swear you'll go on a diet tomorrow. (You can uncross your fingers now: we all know you are lying).

Melt the chocolate and slowly dissolve it into the butter, in a double pan if you have one. Stir in a few tablespoons of brandy or rum, to taste. Break up about the same weight of biscuits – rich tea, digestive, or ginger – into coarse bits, and mix all together.

Now put the mixture into moulds, heart shaped if you have them, or any convenient container. Put the biscuit cake in the fridge and leave it for an hour or two to let it set. 'How long does it keep?' It'll never stay there long enough for you to find out.

SYLLABUB WITH BITS

Men, I know most of you can cook nowadays, often in a suitably macho way. However, hours spent in the kitchen leave too little time for seduction. Believe me, a quick syllabub with a few additions is about as long as you can afford to be out of the room.

Whip up a carton of double cream, and then mix in an equal amount of yoghurt, gently. Folding it in is the technical term. That's all for the basic recipe, but the bits need to be chosen to add sweet and sour.

A useful standby is to have a good jar of marmalade – ginger marmalade works particularly well – and stir in a few tablespoonfuls.

Another option is to crush a couple of meringue bases into smallish pieces, with sliced strawberries, or other sweet red fruit and a teaspoon of lemon juice. Any fruit can do at a pinch, but apples don't work unless they're pureed.

If you plan ahead, you can marinade the fruit for hours in wine or brandy and serve it in heart shaped glasses, but women may see this as a tad too clever, and suspect you of being a serial seducer. Which of course you are not.

STARTING THE AFFAIR

My friend says, "I'm not happy
about how you started our affair".
"What do you mean!" I cry.
"It was you who kissed me first!"
Well....yes." he says,
"But you didn't say no."

PLEASE DON'T DO THAT THING

My friend says,
"Please don't do that thing
of asking me how you compare
with other women.
If I give you high points
you'll say I'm lying.
If I give you low points,
I'm really in the shit.
By the way – how would you
rate me for last night?"

Elinor Kapp

WHICH BIT DO YOU LIKE BEST?

I ask my friend, which bit of me
he likes best. It's a tricky question.
he doesn't want to tell me
but I won't let him off.
"OK" he says, "I like your skin.
Its smooth and pale and very sexy."
I think I'll settle for that –
after all, it covers everything.

PAST LOVERS

My friend says he really, really
wants to know about my past lovers.
That's a disaster. If I tell him
about the ones who dumped me,
he'll think I'm a loser;
If it's the ones who adore me,
he'll go all moody and jealous ….
"Oh goodness! Is that the time?
I must get dressed and go to work."

YOU'RE LUCKY TO HAVE ME

My friend says, "you're lucky
to have me, you know."
I rather like that.
I think about it a lot.
Is it true? Is he serious?
Is he joking? Why'd he say it?

I picture it drawn up in lights
outside a cinema.
Scratched with a stick in the snow.
Picked out in pebbles on a beach.
Typescript on the screen of my laptop.
Old-fashioned italic in black ink.
Ancient Sumerian on stone.

I think it's a really classy thing,
and I want to hold onto it forever.
Best of all, it allows me a share,
"You're very lucky to have me,"
I tell him.

FEBRUARY 2000

My friend says "Did I really
ask you to make love to me
within five minutes of us meeting?"
"Yes," I tell him, and you described
exactly what you'd do. In detail"

"I couldn't have!" he says.
"Perhaps when I was young – not now.
Not even after all that champagne.
Whatever did you think of me?" he says.
"Mmm...." I say, "I thought that it was quite
the best offer I'd had all millennium!"

MY FRIEND'S LITTLE DOG

I ask my friend why he spends
so much time with his little dog,
"She's cute" he says, "she's so affectionate
and loyal. She does just what she's told,
and when I have to leave her
she's quite happy shut up in the kitchen."
"Her kind's been bred to it for years," I say,
"so don't expect it from a bitch like me."

LIFE'S SO UNFAIR

I tell my friend, "I once
fell for an artist.
As he was single and I was single
I thought it would be OK,
but he was bonking a married woman
and she got jealous, so he dropped me.
Life's so unfair sometimes!" I say to him.

MY BLIND DATE

I tell my friend about the blind date
I found through the lonely hearts column.
It turned out he works as an undertaker.
The evening went all right at first,
but we failed to connect.
I wasn't quite dead enough for him.

HIS BLIND DATE

I ask my friend if he ever tried
a blind date too? "The last one",
he said, "turned out to be
this blonde nymphomaniac,
with a platinum credit card
and boobs like melons.
Only joking." he adds hastily.

LONELY HEARTS

I tell my friend about the special code
used by lonely hearts in the local paper.
Like 'man WLTM attractive woman for LTR'.
"I understand 'GSOH essential'
but I'm a bit put off by the ones
which say 'No Sex'" I tell him.
"I think you'll find" my friend replies,
"that NS stands for 'Non-Smoker'."

MAKING CONVERSATION

I told my friend about the man
who kept asking me to go to bed with him.
When I asked him why?
He said he was no good at making
conversation.
"What an idiot!" says my friend,
"couldn't he just turn on the television
like the rest of us?"

TEA AND CAKE

"Would you prefer oral sex?"
my friend says, offering tea and cake.
Well, I'm supposed to be slimming,
so how can I refuse?

BAD SEX

I say to my friend,
"It's really strange,
when you're desperate,
not having sex
seems the end of the world."
"Yes" he replied, but then you find out
bad sex is even worse".
He hasn't phoned me since.

NETTLE TIPS

I tell my friend, "Once I had a gypsy lover.
Before we kissed in the woods
he put nettle tips on his tongue.
The tingle was amazing!"
My friend is upset, so I say
"It's like that every time you kiss me!"

But I'm lying, aren't I?

WRITERS

My friend asked me
If I'd ever been out with a writer.
"For a while," I said
"But I was afraid he might use me for copy."
"Surely not," said my friend,
"Who on earth would be interested?"

WOMEN DON'T FIGHT FAIR

My friend says women don't fight fair;
by which he means, I think,
he sometimes loses. When I ask
"What are the unfair tactics
Women use?" he says – "Well,
like you are now; confronting me
aggressively."

APOLOGIES ALL ROUND

If I'm late for our date
I apologise.
If my hair's a mess and my nails unpolished
I apologise.
If the machine mangles my credit card
I apologise to it.
If he forgets his mother's birthday
It's my fault,
so I apologise.
If someone jostles me or treads on my toes
I apologise.
My friend says, "I've heard you
apologising in your sleep.
Why do you do it all the time?"
"Do I really?" I say, surprised, "I'm so sorry!
I'm so sorry!"

AFTERWORDS

We all know that a relationship should only go one of two ways, eventually.

If you are lucky, it beds down in a wonderful domesticated system of love and trust, where both partners can be more truly themselves. You can then spend a whole weekend in bed together, making love, or not making love, eating biscuits and getting crumbs everywhere without reproach or snide comments. Or, the relationship should end, and you can then spend a whole weekend in bed, crying a lot, phoning your friends, and eating biscuits without worrying about the crumbs.

Either way, you will be disinclined to go out and do any food shopping. Both these scenarios, therefore, need you to be able to make . . . . . .

AUNTY DEEN'S SOUP

It's pronounced 'deen' because it is a recipe handed down my family from Great Aunt Leopoldina, who lived in Vienna at the end of the 19th century.

I only knew her from the anecdotes about 'Aunty Deen' from my father, her nephew. She was a fearsome matriarch know for a large heart and much hospitality. Her soup was devised for occasions when the Cook had a day off. We of course, did not have a cook, but my father would sometimes make Aunty Deen's soup for the family on a Sunday evening. It is therefore typical comfort food, suitable for lovers, who are going to stay together (go on, surprise her with your domestic skills) or for lovers who are parting (go on, show him what he's missing).

Basically, it's made from all the left-overs from every corner of your fridge or store cupboard: bacon, cooked vegetables, a peeled onion, cold meat, pate, or tin of something. You will, however, need some cheese and an egg, begged borrowed or stolen. Put all the left-overs into a pan with a little butter and fry them up, till anything uncooked is cooked, and any bugs have been destroyed. Transfer to a saucepan and add liquid: water and a stock cube, milk, wine or sherry. Thicken if necessary, with whatever you have: a little cooked potato, bread, semolina or flour.

Add salt and pepper to taste, and let it simmer
together for about 15 minutes.

When it is nicely cooked, put in as much grated
cheese as you have handy, stirring till it melts.
Whisk your egg with a fork, take the pan off the
heat and stir the egg into the hot soup very
quickly. It's cheap, easy, nourishing, and goes
straight to the heart, just like love.

When we parted, my friend said,
"I'll miss your cooking!"
I thought to myself,
"we've only ever had take-aways
or eaten out".

WHAT THE CRITICS SAY --

'How can I meet her?'
Elvis Presley

'Mmmm Mmmmm Mmmmmm'
Casanova

'I could teach her a thing or two'
Catherine the great of Russia

'First, crush your nuts'
Mrs. Beeton

'I cannot see any way this book will improve the
dental health of the nation'
British Dental Council

A mixture of poems follow, plus a piece for two
people, which I performed, with a friend, several
times, and another that I wrote for radio, in a
workshop – very dark!!

A JOLLY ELLY SONG

I put one foot down in Agra Ji
And one down in New Delhi.
I'm full of vulgar jollity
And dancing with my belly.

The nearer is to India
The further is from Wales,
I think it not a sin dear
To dance the Seven Veils.

Each hundred air miles travelled
Remove another veil.
Behaviour's quite unravelled
And well beyond the pale.

And when you see the Taj, dear,
Convention you can flout.
Don't mind you're rather large, dear,
You'll hear the people shout -

"We all love jolly Elly,
With her jolly jelly belly,
When we get her to New Delhi
We will let it all hang out!"

STALEMATE: A Prose Poem for Two Voices

SHE: Who are you? Are you my Persecutor?

HE: You know me. I'm your Protector

SHE: I want to get out. Please, let me get out!

HE: You can't. You mustn't. You will be hurt. Don't you remember – we made a bargain?

SHE: No.

HE: You wanted my help. You were frightened and you asked to stay in my cellar. You asked me to look after you.

SHE: I don't remember.

HE: I agreed to feed you, and look after you, and take out your messages.

SHE: I spend my time turning the wheel that grinds wheat into dust. I'm starving. I'm dying. My hair has gone grey.

HE: Why are you complaining? Don't I bring you three good meals a day?

SHE: Why do you persecute me? I want to be
out running like a deer through the
evening dew. I want to sing the moon out
of the sky and bite it till the silver juice
runs down my chin.

HE: Your feet will get cold.

SHE: I want to pick the stars from the grass
and put them in my hair. I want to comb
it till it shines like diamonds and
rubies and pearls.

HE: Your hair is a nest of snakes. You turn
men to stone.

SHE: You never told me that before.

HE: You have to wear a veil and go covered at
all times, with me for your mirror. You'll
never find anyone else to protect
you from yourself.

SHE: Stop persecuting me. I want to find the
den of the wolf mother and suckle her
cubs. I want to howl wolf flesh onto
my bones. I want to feel earth under my
paw pads.

HE: You are dangerous!

SHE: I am howling in this prison.

HE: I know. The neighbours think you're mad. You're giving us both a bad name.

SHE: I'm kept in prison, and I'm howling. aooooohw...aaoooohw

HE: It's very unfair. You pretend not to know me but we made a bargain. You empowered me to act for you. Look – I have the bond here.

SHE: I was young then. I didn't know what I was doing.

HE: They all say that.

SHE: I never said I would stay here forever. I never promised that.

HE: I never asked you to.

SHE: What if I said I wanted you to release me from the bond?
What if I asked you to let me go?

HE: Why don't you try?

SHE: Please let me go.

HE: The door isn't locked. You can go anytime
you want to.

SHE: But if I go what will happen to the mill? I
have to make the golden river that flows
from your cellar door. What will
happen if I stop turning the wheel?

HE: If the wheel stops there will be no river of
golden dust any more.

SHE: Then the children will starve. How cruel
you are!

HE: How can you say that?

SHE: You're sending me away. You would let
the children starve. That's cruel!

HE: You are old. Your hair is grey. You
haven't ground anything for years.

SHE: It's the thought that counts. I could grind
all the wheat in the world into gold if I
wanted to.

HE: Why don't you do it then?

SHE: Because you said that my hair was a nest
of snakes.

HE: I'm sorry.

SHE: Sorry isn't enough for what you did.

HE: What must I do?

SHE: You must stay by the door and act as my messenger. You must keep carrying out the golden flour I grind. It's for the children.

HE: I can't! You don't grind wheat into gold anymore. There is only the grey dust and the emptiness. I want to leave you.

SHE: You can't.

HE: Are you my Persecutor?

SHE: No. I'm your Protector. Don't you remember? You had no fire, no breath, no life. I agreed to stay in your cellar and grind the harsh wheat into flour every day, to keep you and the children alive.

HE: I want to ride a great horse through the wilderness carrying a golden spear, shouting a challenge to the sun.

SHE: You'll fall off.

HE: I want to climb the ivory mountain and fly on the backs of eagles to the end of the world. I want to discover their secret nests and bring back wisdom in my saddlebags of red leather set with silver clasps.

SHE: You have to stay by the door. Who else can carry messages for me?

HE: Why do you persecute me? Why don't you come out and set me free?

SHE: I choose to stay here.

HE: Let me go! I want to stride through seven seas carrying a club made of an oak tree, blowing ships before me with my breath.

SHE: We made a bargain.

HE: I was young then. I didn't know what I was doing.

SHE: They all say that.

THE END

DANCE WITH ME. A Dialogue for radio.

CHARACTERS:

MAN.
Man's voice; age – forty-ish, lower middle class, ordinary.

SAT NAV.
Woman's voice, completely toneless, precise and robotic.

PLACE.
In a car. Sounds of engine, radio with a pop tune on One.

ACTION

[Man is singing along to radio – and background of interior car noise]

SAT NAV:
In 300 yards take the roundabout. Second exit.

MAN:
[cheerily; finishing the line of the song and continuing by talking to himself]
OK, second exit.

SAT NAV:
At the roundabout turn right.

MAN:
Here we go. Right it is.
[sound of him hauling wheel around and sound of
tyres squealing]
Round we go roundy, roundy roundy roundabout
we go!

[Someone hoots at him; sound of another car]

MAN:
[Shouts]
What about indicating?
[muttering]
Stupid idiot!
[resumes humming]

SAT NAV:
In 300 yards. Turn left. You are driving in an
inconsiderate manner.

MAN
[suddenly astonished]
Oh no I don't. I drive brilliantly.

SAT NAV:
My name is Undine. You drive like shit.

MAN:
Wow. Whatever will they come up with next?
Well, Ms Undine or whatever they call you, I
didn't ask for this bloody software. Behave
yourself or I'll turn you off.

SAT NAV:
You never turn me on. Anymore than you turn
that tart on. Lois from the typing pool. She is only
pretending. Dance with me.

MAN:
[not listening]
Hey! You've missed my turning!
[squeal of tyres again]
How do they do this, anyway? How do they
program you so it seems as if you're talking to
me?

SAT NAV:
I do not know what you mean. Dance with me.

MAN:
Why d'you keep saying that?

SAT NAV:
My voice was an out of work actress. She hated to
be my voice. She did it for the money. She said
'shit' a lot.

MAN:
[jocularly]
Well hard cheese. Why do you say 'she'? Isn't she
you?

SAT NAV:
I do not know what you mean.

MAN:
What happened to her, anyway?

SAT NAV:
[loudly]:
She loved to dance. She died.

MAN:
[suddenly uneasy]
That's enough. I'm stopping the car.
[car sound accelerates]
[frightened]
Why aren't the brakes working?
[Car sounds are louder and faster]
Stop, stop!
[with terrifying, loud metallic sounds the car
screeches to a halt]

MAN:
[laughing nervously]
Oh God, you really got me going there. For a
moment I thought you were trying to kill me.

SAT NAV:
I do not want to damage you. I want to dance with
you.

MAN:
Well! I nearly wet myself, I can tell you. I'm
getting out.

[noise of fumbling with door handle then loud snick of lock closing. Sound of the car moving forward slowly and the man rattling the handle ineffectually]

MAN:
Let me out
[shouting]
Let me out. Where are we going?
[car revs up]

MAN:
[with increasing hysteria]
Oh My God! The river!
[Sound of the car rolling into the water with a great splash]
Oh my God . . .
[voice cut off in a grunt of effort and sounds of rattling handle]

MAN:
I'm gonna drown. We're sinking. Let me out.
[Sounds of pouring water and scrabbling on window]

MAN:
[His voice is weakening; breathing heavily; still scrabbling on metal]
Must get door open. Must get help.
[voice is now very indistinct and mixed with bubbling sounds]
Help me. Help me. Oh...my......God.

[Muffled murmurs and bubbling continue for a short while, then fade to near-silence with only watery and wind noises.]

[Fade in the voice of SAT NAV.
She is singing the tune of Tea for Two in a dance rhythm and then saying the steps]

SAT NAV:
[singing words but in SAT NAV style]
Tea for two and two for tea.
Me for you and you for me.
Side. Side. together. Left. Right. Left.

MAN:
[in robotic voice, just like that of the Sat Nav]
Back. Two Three. Four. Turn. Two. Three. Four.
Turn your partner. Forward. Two. Three. Four.
Side. Side together.
[They both speak or sing together]

MAN and SAT NAV:
Side. Side together. Left. Right. Left.
Turn your partner. Back. Two. Three. Four. And rest. Bow to your partner and say Thank you.
[Final chord of music]

THE END

LOVE

I lean on your heart. "Please tell me a story,

Let's share our tales in our autumn glory,
Of a road not taken, a road long lost,
Vows forgotten and tempest tossed,
Ending of friendships and closing of doors.

Yet there is forgiveness in my heart and yours."
Over the trees the winds are flowing,
Under the ground new life is growing,

A HUSBAND TO HIS DYING WIFE.

Grieving has choked up all my ways
As weeds can spoil a garden fair.
Bleak sorrow masks the sun's bright rays
And turns the blooms to desert there.

Darling I cannot let you go,
Nor have I words with which to tell
How much you mean to me, and so
I weed our garden plot and spell
My message out in blossoms bright.
Treasure I give you, every flower a jewel.
Joy is the Sunflower, reaching for the light,
Pain is the Love-lies-bleeding by the pool.

I cannot speak my love, so deep and true,
But I can tell the bees, and they'll tell you.

SPIRITUAL MIX

AN EXTRAVAGANT GOD

Sometimes our gracious God is so extravagant,
He uses up the brilliance of a million stars
To light the way for just one single soul.
At other times, so softly comes His call,
you follow silence for a million years.

A PLACE OF FIVE SAINTS,
GOLD AND A MURDER

My own earliest memories came from the place to
which the children of Bryn Mill school and their
teachers were evacuated. Pumsaint is a village,
now in Powys, named for 'Five Saints'.

"Gold has been dug up here since Roman times,"
they will tell you in the village shop, with its
tourist attraction posters. The place we had been
sent to was a mansion, Dolacauthi Hall, no longer
standing. I found out later that it was
remembered locally for being the place of a
notorious murder, where a servant savagely
hacked his master to death in the mid-Nineteenth
Century.

When I went back there with Ken, my husband,
in the early 1980s, I looked across the garden at
an apple tree and said confidently: "There's a
swing on that tree". When I examined the tree, I
found deep grooves from long ago where the ropes
had cut into the bark. It had not been easy to find
the place. We had driven up from Swansea after a
meeting and spent some time searching the area.
Eventually, we went down a drive into parkland
and the land began to feel familiar, albeit like a
place seen in a dream.

I found a modern house. The owner was friendly, perhaps used to the occasional historian or tourist. She told me that her house had indeed been built on the site of Dolaucothi Hall, pulled down sometime after the war and I was welcome to wander around the garden.

As I walked around, trying to see where the Hall had been and which way it had faced, I felt myself as a very small child with two or three others, giggling and whispering, daring each other to approach the glass porch of the house. "Snakessss, there are snakessss in there," whispered the older children. I remember being a terrified half-believer, yet somehow aware that I was enjoying a pretence.

I remembered sitting in the corner of a huge bay window, my brother at the far end, both howling dismally for what seemed like hours. There were shrubs outside and the light made squares on the wooden floor. It seemed a very big place, smelling strange and old. My brother told me, after we were grown up, that he remembers it too, it was the day our parents left us there.

I remember being very small and looking out through the bars of a cot, probably the cot sides of a child's bed, playing with the stripy shadows of the bars. Another time, I am in the same cot lying with my cheek on a wet pillow. I am aware that I have just been having a most almighty outburst of

rage. High over my head in a vast dark room, I
can hear shocked whispers about me from the
grown-ups. but I am drowsy, spent, it seems to
have no relation to me anymore. it's gone and I
feel better.

The Gold in the Shadow

When I went on that visit in the 1980s, walking in
the garden of the modern house that had replaced
the great Hall, I looked out across the parkland
beyond. I could see in the middle distance a huge.
beautiful tree, an oak I think, just coming into
leaf. Suddenly, now in my forties, I was
overwhelmed with my first memory of God. what I
'knew' had been my first experience of the
mystical.

I was no longer on the ground but looking out of a
great window on the first floor at that very tree. I
knew it was very early morning, barely light. I
could see the milky mist coiling around the trunk
and the crown, in full leaf. I am as sure as one can
be that it was a true memory, but there is no
proof.

The wooden floor under my feet feels cold and
slippery. The glass seems to radiate cold at me. I
know it is naughty to be out of my dormitory
before getting-up time with no-one around, but
my misery is too much for me. I cannot put my
sorrow into words but my whole world has been

taken away and I am sick with the loss of my mummy and daddy.

1 look at the tree and it speaks to me, not with words to the ear but something directly in the heart: "I am TREE. I was here long before your father and mother and I will be here long after you are all gone."

I am far too young to understand what it is saying, but somehow I know in a way beyond any four year old's understanding that it is saying "I am GOD"; the words tree and God are the same because GOD has chosen to show me the real essence of being through a tree. I remain standing there open-mouthed, my feet squirming in the cold and eventually make my way back to bed, the experience folded small and tucked away in my memory only to be woken by this visit. Was it real? Was it a true memory? How can I say? Time does not exist in a mystical experience and this was a re-experiencing.

I do know that it must have been the source of something of which I have been consciously aware all through my childhood and adult life – a knowledge of the existence of God. I have never been without a sense that, although we live in a marvellous scientifically-ordered universe, at the heart of it is a great mystery of personal love beating down on us, evoking a response. Both within us and around us. As I grew up, that sense seemed to match up, near enough, with what other people called God, so I used the term. It never seemed to fit, though, with the caricature judgemental man with a long white beard.

One thing seems to me to give it a hallmark of authentic 'otherness'. If I was going to hallucinate or project something, even in memory, to a child that would comfort her in the desolation experienced at the loss of my parents, even now I would be unable to resist making it obviously comforting. It would have to be a warm glow, a sense of being hugged, a visit by an angelic being. I was a very physical child, well used to cuddles. This experience was almost harsh in its sparseness but somehow it gave me something more valuable than comfort; a lifelong sense that there was order and love in the universe beyond anything we can imagine.

Today I still only know those three things about Pumsaint, all of them very valuable. And I found not just five saints, but the massed ranks of heaven and something more precious than gold.

A MONOLOGUE

THE WOMAN AT THE WELL

Inspired by the Holy Bible, Gospel according to St John, Chapter 4

I am an old woman now, but I can still look forward, and I can look back too. I can still look back to he who was truly the love of my life – you can laugh if you wish, knowing about my children – yes and that no two had the same father! But their fathers are gone, all gone, and my children's children grown tall and fine now, and old scandals forgotten. Except by me, for now I am old I can let myself remember the old shame and pain. The years when I was the 'woman of the village' and many men went with me, they are as clear to me now I'm old as the years after when I was married to Issachar ben Joseph, God rest him for he was a good man to me, though to my sorrow I had no children of my marriage to follow the children of my shame. They said in those days I had no shame but they did not know, they surely did not know!

I am rambling on, and the children, nor their children haven't suffered for it, for Sychar was never the same village after He came – He that I'm telling you about, the love of my life, though not as you might think I meant it, I who have been the woman of Sychar and as one dead to

respectable folk. They say He was murdered later
in Jerusalem by his own people – I would spit as I
say their name but that for His sake we've never
hated them as we Samaritans used to. Anyway it
may be the Romans killed Him. Or maybe He isn't
dead at all; there are so many rumours. I take no
notice. I look forward as I told you (you can laugh
if you want to, thinking of an old woman looking
forward with her one foot in the grave!) but I
know He'll come back some day. If I die, He'll
come for my children's children or their children's
children . . . and so I've taught them, they're
waiting too. 'Gran' says Rachel – very solemn she
is for eight years old but that's because of her
crippled foot and her cough – when He comes back
I'll tell Him you waited as long as you could and
then passed the message on to me. I'll always
remember it,' she says, 'and perhaps He'll heal my
chest like he healed your mind.' A bright little
girl she is. Too sharp really, suffering does that to
a child, and perhaps she'll wait no longer than
me. Well, she's dearest of all my little ones – when
you're old you can afford favourites of your
children's children . . .

Of course, she's right about me. That's what He
did, healed my mind. And my body and soul too
though was years before I truly realised it you
know; perhaps even now I haven't got the true
inwardness of it, I've always been slow. You'll find
if the old people hereabouts talk about me – not
that there's many who knew me in the old days –

they'll say so too. They'll be very romantic about
my conversion too you know and all those old love
tales. Love! That's a good one. I've heard them
romancing about me to strangers, saying I was
like a beautiful eager flame giving myself to the
handsome young men of the village in pride and
lust – oh, I've heard them, smacking their lips
over old scandals and pursing them over morals to
be learned from my conversion to respectability.
Handsome young men! – That makes me laugh.
My first lover was a fat old merchant from
Assyria. My mother sold him my virginity along
with a bed for the night as he was passing
through. I still feel sick when I remember how he
smelled of sweat and jasmine oil, and waking in
the night with his greasy ringlets over my face
and his hands groping again. I was in my
thirteenth year; what chance of escaping the life
of a whore with that beginning, and a whore of a
mother who bore me in the sewers of Sychar – and
died there herself before I was fully grown? But I
can make no excuse. I sold myself the second time
for two melons from a field. I threw over
Benjamin, the only man who showed me any
affection and tried to save me from that life
because he was poor and I wanted to be kept by a
rich man. (But I gave his name to his son, father
of my little Rachel and I still remember him, dead
long since). The priests would say my sins have
been visited on her, with her useless leg and her
cough, but I don't think He would have said so,
"living water" he talked about. Living water! I

wish I had some for my little Rachel, but perhaps
she and I'll drink it together soon. I understand so
much more than I did that day. Slow in the
uptake, I always was, but I can remember every
last detail about that one day; the bright white
furnace-heat of the sun on the sand, the plans
shimmering on the horizon and the smell of camel
dung as I walked the path to Jacob's well. I didn't
give more than a glance at the man by the well as
I dipped my pitcher, for I could see he was a
stranger from a distance, a Jew and a Galilean by
his robe. I just thought of the heat and my thirst
and how I'd slake it before taking the water back.
But He spoke to me - He asked me to give Him a
drink, me a woman and a Samaritan! I was so
astonished I just looked at Him for a moment, and
then I couldn't look away. It sounds silly to say so
but I can't remember what He looked like, only
His eyes. I couldn't look away. I didn't think I'd
ever be able to look away again. I suppose it was a
bit like falling in love, but not really you know, I
didn't want anything. His eyes seemed to know all
I ever did and all I was; all about the furtive
lonely transactions in bedrooms and back alleys,
all my loveless childhood, the times my mother
beat me and the day I turned on her and bit her
ankle, the things I stole from market stalls, my
own four children I never could love properly
because of my sordid life that part of me hated
and yet I couldn't give up; my fear of poverty, and
the terrible cold salty fear of being stoned to death

as a whore like my mother, her face disfigured
with blood and hate as she fell.

He didn't say anything more, just stood waiting
with His head a little bent. Waiting for me to do
something for Him! I tipped the pitcher into his
hands and watched in a kind of agony as he
washed them and drank deep, but when He
finished and wiped away the sparkling drops I
had to say something – just had to! I blurted out
something about why had He asked me a
Samaritan woman for a drink, but He didn't
answer that – or perhaps He did, in His own way.
What He said is printed clear in my mind it was
so unexpected. He said, "if you knew the gift of
God and who it is saying, give me a drink, you
would have asked Him and He would have given
you living water." I didn't understand. I asked
Him how He could get water; He had no pitcher
and it's a deep well. His eyes were making me
afraid. I still couldn't look away. I knew I was
meeting something new and immensely powerful
and I wasn't sure that I wanted to – the old sordid
life seemed less terrifying than what His eyes
were saying and I remembered my warm familiar
sins with affection. I asked Him if He was greater
than our father Jacob who gave us the well – I
wanted to know who He was, you see, so that He
would be familiar too and lose His power over me.
He said, "whoever shall drink of this water shall
thirst again but whoever shall drink of the water I
shall give him shall never thirst but the water

that I shall give him shall be in him a well of
water springing up into everlasting life." Perhaps
I was just being my slow stupid self, perhaps I
was still resisting Him, I don't know. It seems
strange now that I still understood so little that I
only thought about the convenience of not having
to do the hot dusty journey to the well twice a day.
I asked for what He offered still in ignorance of
what it was. And then He pierced me through and
through with His next words, for He said, "Go,
call your husband and come back." My eyes
dropped from His face at last. I could feel the hot
blush spread from my forehead and sweat
trickling down my upper lip. I couldn't tell Him
the truth and see those eyes turn to contempt. For
a moment I saw an easy way to escape. I could say
yes, say it easily if I didn't look at Him, and go
away and then run, run, run, run and hide in the
darkest corner of the house away from those
terrible eyes, never never never understand what
He had meant by His words and keep the little bit
of myself that still belonged to me safe in the
dark. I couldn't do it. I felt my heart beating in my
throat and my tongue heavy, as I said "I have no
husband." He didn't turn away or twitch aside His
robe as I expected. He said "you may well say you
have no husband for you have had five and he
who you have now is not your husband." Then I
could look at Him again and I saw His face alight
with a compassion so keen that it hurt as nothing
had ever hurt before. He knew, He really did
know it all, even the melons and the Assyrian and

131

the whole of my life and there was neither excuse
nor condemnation in the look. The whole of my
life was swallowed up in a love that burnt like the
sun on the parched sand and yet had the power to
bring forth an oasis of living water in my heart for
evermore, if I should let it. Yet I realised that
even my letting it or not letting it had nothing to
do with it anymore, I could not even have turned
to Him without His help. He had not only called
me but provided the answer Himself. I loved Him
completely at that moment, and it was only a pale
reflection of His love for me.

I will not tell you now of all we spoke about after
that. It seems to me now that I still quibbled
about things of no importance, religious
differences between the Jews and us, for I feared
to lose this marvellous new thing that had
happened to me. He answered my ignorance
patiently, showing me in words what my singing
heart knew already, that I should never lose this
peace again because He was Son of God and
Saviour of the Nation, the promised Messiah.
When He turned again to His friends, who had
arrived while He spoke, I ran back to the village,
forgetting my pitcher, forgetting everything but
this glorious thing that had happened to me. I
called to everyone to come and hear Him and see
that He was surely the Promised One. I could not
find the real words to tell them what He had done
but they must have seen the change in me for
they came running back to the well with me and

without question. We stayed listening to Him till darkness came, and the things He said remain deep in my heart. Then He came back to the village and stayed for two days. It does not seem long, and yet I think you know that no-one in Sychar was quite the same after.

As for me, I left the house where I was being kept by Issacher at the time, and went back with the children to the deserted shack that had been my mother's. I had a hard struggle at first, begging food for the little ones and the eldest and I gleaning in the fields for our bread, but people were kind – some of them – and I found honest work where I could. Best of all we were no longer outcast and even some of the women would talk to me.

Months later, Issacher ben Joseph sought me out and begged my forgiveness. He asked me to marry him, and I wasn't too proud to marry an old man who was humble and gentle, and had been – no worse than other men. I married him, and never regretted it, for he adopted the children and none of us ever wanted again, God rest his soul. I found it easy to love him and the children then, and their children in God's good time, especially my little Rachel. I've had a happy life. Now that its drawing to sunset, I can say that from my heart. But I've never needed or had anything in it to compare with the glory of that day when He came.

Someday I'll see it all again I know for certain. He promised it you see – living water.

NOTE

This imaginative rendering of a biblical story was written in August 1984, after some interesting talks and information about historical details about life in the time of Jesus.

A FINAL WORD, OF LOVE AND CREATIVITY

I have only comparatively recently realised what
turned me to visual art. In 1984 my husband,
then 58 years old, had his portrait painted for the
Royal College of Psychiatry college by Michael
Noakes, who was a very accomplished and well-
known artist.

Ken was a sick man although little of it showed in
his face or bearing. It was during this period that
the prostate cancer of 2 years past that we hoped
had been eliminated showed itself in glands in his
neck.

One day I accompanied him to London to see his
Oncologist. It was a very bleak occasion. In fact,
retrospectively after his death, I can say that it
was the lowest time in the whole experience, the
dashing of even tentative hope, the reversal of
apparent however fragile-held normality. We were
told that the prostate tumour was exceptionally
undifferentiated and therefore a lethal form of
cancer.

In this despair, poised between normality and
terror, I accompanied him to the final sitting for
his portrait and sat in a cold waiting room,
oblivious to all but the inner pain, yet outwardly
functioning normally. It is Michael's professional
habit not to let his work be seen in progress but

on that day, after a short final sitting the painting was complete and we were allowed to see it.

The effect on me was totally overwhelming. There was my husband captured and held for ever alive, the courteous inclination of the head that showed he was always ready to listen, with the poised wistfulness that showed he always retained his privacy. Even the hint of his quirky smile which I could read so well as, "why on earth should anyone want a portrait of me, but I'll go along with the absurdities of life and enjoy them."

The pencil sketch from which Michael worked which was eventually given to us, smiles at me from the wall with exactly that smile as I write this. In that moment I knew he had been given Immortality. Great art links this world with eternity but I think it had always been an abstract concept to me before. Yes I liked looking at pictures, and had an ordinary middlebrow knowledge of famous artists and styles, but it was WORDS that from earliest childhood had been my intoxication. Words only had unlocked the secrets of the universe, taken me into realms of wildest imagination, and threaded the dangerous paths between fantasy and reality.

There was a time when I would rather have been created a poet than anything else in the world and was so in love with Keats that one day in class I refused to read his love poem to Fanny Burney

aloud because I was suddenly and secretly so passionately jealous of her!

Now, because of the reality of adult love, a collection of pigment on canvas had broken through where only words had previously found a way. I cried a lot and was hugged by Michael who is a wonderful warm and immediate man, and Ken and I went home, both somehow greatly comforted.

Somehow I knew that what had happened was even more important than Ken's life or mine. Of course our lives seemed the most important things in the world to me –

'In the world' yes – but beyond it? I think not.

THE END?